# Physics

NCERT: Class 12

Last ten minutes before exam

Z. Fetcher

Assistant Professor

Research, Education & Training

## Preface

This book is good and meant for students preparing for CBSE exam and exams that follow NCERT syllabus. As we all know that Physics is an integral component of general education at all 10+2 level. This book has been written strictly is accordance with the latest syllabus issued by CBSE/NCERT.

## MAIN FEATURES OF THE BOOK

- Briefly discussed subject matter.
- A judicious use of table, and illustrations to make the subjects matter lucid, clear and interesting.
- Simple, lucid and student–friendly language is used.
- Strictly in accordance with the latest syllabus.

  I have tried my level best to present the subject matter precisely, practically and correctly but errors have the habits of creeping in inadvertently.

  I do hope that the readers and the teachers will send their valuable suggestion to make the book more useful and praise worthy.

Z. Fetcher

Author

## Contents

### After reading this book you will be able to

- define the terms frequently asked in Electrostatics, Electrostatic potential and

capacitance, current electricity and ray optics and optical instruments
- SI units used in Electrostatics, Electrostatic potential and capacitance, current electricity and ray optics and optical instruments
- write and answer short questions

## Introduction

In this book, you will be able to know about the types of charges that we come across or experience in our daily life like seeing a spark or hearing a crackle or rubbing of insulating surfaces. Also, you will be able to know and learn about the electromagnetic waves within a small range of electromagnetic spectrum (wave length of about 400nm to 750 nm) to which the human eye is sensitive and able to detect.

Here you will be able to learn and know about the terminologies used in electro statics, capacitance, potential energy, static charges and charges in motion and ray optics, their SI units and reasoning questions that are frequently asked in exams.

**Some important terminologies are as under:**

**A**

**What do you mean by additivity of charges?**

**Additivity of charges**

Additivity of charges means the total charge on a system is the algebraic sum (with proper signs) of all individual charges in the system.

# B

## What is a beam of light?

## Beam of light

- Beam of light refers to a group of light rays.
- A light beam or beam of light refers to a directional projection of light energy radiating from a light source.
- Beam of light refers to the collection or bunch of light rays emitted from a luminous body.
- Sunlight forms a light beam when filtered through media such as clouds, foliage or windows.

# C

## What is classical Physics?

**Classical Physics**

- Classical Physics is a group of Physics theories that predate modern, more complete or more widely applicable theories.
- Classical Physics refers to Physics not involving quantum mechanics or the theory of relativity. It is opposed to experimental Physics.

**What are conductors?**

**Conductors**

Conductors are substances which allow electricity to pass through them easily.

**What do you mean by charging by contact?**

**Charging by contact**

Charging by contact refers to the process of giving one object a net electric charge by placing it in contact with another object that is already charged. For example, electrons are transferred by rubbing the negatively charged rod on the metal sphere.

## What do you mean by charging by induction?

## Charging by induction

Induction charging is a method used to charge an object without actually touching the object to any other charged object.

## What do you mean by charge is conserved?

## Charge conservation

- In Physics, charge conservation is the principle that the total electric charge in an isolated system never changes.
- The net quantity of electric charge, the amount of positive charge minus the amount of negative charge in the universe, is always conserved.

## Define 1 Coulomb of charge.

# 1 Coulomb of charge

One (1) Coulomb of charge is the charge flowing through a wire in 1 second(s) if the current is 1 A (Ampere).

## What are corpuscles in terms of optics?

## Corpuscles

In optics, the corpuscular theory of light states that light is made up of small discrete particles called "corpuscles" (little particles) which travel in a straight line with a finite velocity and passes impetus.

## What is a capacitor?

## Capacitor

- A capacitor is a system of two conductors separated by an insulator.
- A single conductor can be considered as capacitor with other conductor at infinity.
- The total charge of a capacitor is zero while the conductors have charge q and − q.

## What is capacitance?

## Capacitance

- Capacitance refers to the ratio of the electric charge on each conductor to the potential difference (i.e voltage) between them.
- $C=q/V$ The constant C is called the capacitance of the capacitor.

## What do you mean by capacitors in series?

## Capacitors in series

- When capacitors are connected one after another, they are said to be in series.
- When capacitors are connected in series, the total capacitance is less than any one of the series capacitors individual capacitances.
- The total potential drop V across the combination is the sum of the potential drops $V_1$ and $V_2$ across $C_1$ and $C_2$ respectively.

$$V = V_1 + V_2 = q/C_1 + q/C_2$$
$$V/q = 1/C_1 + 1/C_2$$
$$C = q/V \text{ or } 1/C = V/q$$
$$1/C = 1/C_1 + 1/C_2$$

**What do you mean by capacitors in parallel?**

**Capacitors in parallel**

- Capacitors are connected together in parallel when both of its terminals are connected to each terminal of another capacitor.
- The voltage ($V_c$) connected across all the capacitors that are connected in parallel is the same.

$$C = C_1 + C_2 + C_3 + \ldots \ldots C_n$$

**What do you mean by current density?**

**Current density**

Current per unit area (taken normal to the current), I/A is called current density and is denoted by j.

**What are carbon resistors?**

**Carbon resistors**

- Carbon resistors are compact, inexpensive and thus find extensive use in electronic circuits.
- Carbon resistors are small in size and hence their values are given using a colour code.
- The first two bands from the end indicate the first two significant figures of the resistance in Ohms.
- The third band indicates the decimal multiplier.
- The last band stands for tolerance or possible variation in percentage about the indicated values.

**What is critical angle?**

**Critical angle**

In optics, critical angle refers to the greatest angle at which a ray of light, travelling in one transparent medium, can strike the boundary between that medium and a second of lower refractive index without being totally reflected within the first medium.

**What are convergent rays?**

**Convergent rays**

Convergent rays refer to light rays that come together (converges) after reflection and refraction at a single point known as the focus.

**What is chromatic aberration?**

**Chromatic aberration**

When white light passes through thick lenses, red and blue colours focus at different points. This phenomenon is known as chromatic aberration.

**What do you mean by combination of resistors in parallel?**

**Combination of resistors in parallel**

Two or more resistors are said to be in parallel if one end of all the resistors is joined together and similarly the other ends joined together.

# D

**Define a dipole.**

**Dipole**

A dipole is a pair of opposite charges with equal magnitude separated by a distance (d).

**What is diffused reflection of light?**

**Diffused reflection**

Diffused reflection refers to the reflection of light from a surface such that an incident ray is reflected at many angles.

**What is dielectric?**

## Dielectric

Dielectric refers to the insulating material or a very poor conductor of electric current. When dielectrics are placed in an electric field, practically no current flows in them because, unlike metals, they have no loosely bound or free electrons that may drift through the material.

## What is dielectric polarization?

## Dielectric polarization

Dielectric polarization refers to the behaviour of a material when an external electric field is applied on it.

## Define dioptre.

## Dioptre

The power of a lens of focal length of one meter is one dioptre.

## What is drift velocity?

## Drift velocity

- When particles like electrons attain the average velocity under the influence of an electric field is known as the drift velocity.
- Drift velocity is the average velocity attained by charged particles, such as electrons, in a material due to an electric field.

Formula, $V_d = I/neA$   where

$V_d$ is the drift velocity

I is the current flow

n is the free electron density

e is the charge of an electron

A is the cross sectional area

**What are divergent rays?**

**Divergent rays**

Divergent rays are light rays from a point source of light travel in all directions, moving away with time.

## What is angle of deviation in a prism?

- The angle between the incident ray and emergent ray is called the angle of deviation.
- The smallest angle through which light is bent by an optical element or a system.
- Angle of deviation refers to emergent ray is bent at an angle with the direction of the incident ray.

## What is dispersion of light?

## Dispersion of light

Dispersion of light refers to the process of splitting of white light into seven colours. For example, formation of a rainbow during a cloudy day.

## E

## What is electrostatics?

## Electrostatics

- Electrostatics is a branch of Physics that studies electric charges at rest.
- Electrostatics deals with the study of forces, fields and potential arising from static charges.
- Electrostatics is the study of forces between charges, as described by Coulomb's law.
- Electrostatics is the study of electromagnetic phenomenon that occurs when there are no moving charges i.e after a static equilibrium has been established.
- Electrostatics is the branch of Physics that deals with phenomenon due to attractions or repulsions of electric charges but not dependent upon their motion.

**What does electrostatic force mean?**

**Electrostatic force**

Electrostatic force also called Coulomb force or Coulomb interaction, attraction or repulsion of particles or objects because of their electric charge.

**What is electrostatic shielding?**

**Electrostatic shielding**

- Electrostatic shielding refers to the phenomenon of making a region free from electric field or its partial component.

- Any cavity of any shape and size is always shielded from outer electric influence. This is called electrostatic shielding. The field inside the cavity is always zero.

**What is electric charge?**

**Electric charge**

- Electric charge refers to the basic property of matter carried by some elementary particles that governs how the particles are affected by an electric or magnetic field.

- Electric charge, which can be positive or negative, occurs in discrete natural units and is neither created nor destroyed.
- Electric charge or charge is the quantity of unbalanced electricity in a body (either positive or negative).
- Electric charge is the physical property of matter that causes it to experience a force when placed in an electromagnetic field.

**What is an electroscope?**

**Electroscope**

Electroscope is an instrument used to detect the presence of electric charge on a body.

**What do you mean by an electric dipole?**

**Electric dipole**

- An electric dipole deals with the separation of the positive and negative charges found in any electromagnetic system.

- An electric dipole is a type of electric charge distribution which contains two point charges, one positive and one negative.
- An electric dipole is a combination of two point charges having equal magnitude but opposite signs.
- The total charge of the electric dipole – the two charges in a dipole have the same magnitude, so the net charge of the dipole is zero.

**What do you mean by electric field?**

**Electric field**

- An electric field refers to an electric property associated with each point in space when charge is present in any form.
- Electric field is defined as the electric force per unit charge.
- An electric field is the physical field that surrounds each electric charge and exerts force on all other charges in the field, either attracting or repelling them.

- The magnitude and direction of the electric field are expressed by the value of E called electric field strength or electric field intensity or simply the electric field.

**What is electric potential?**

**Electric potential**

The electric potential at a point in free space due to a charge 'q' coulomb is $E = 4\pi\epsilon_0$ q x $10^{22}$Vm$^{-1}$.

**What are electric field lines?**

**Electric field lines**

- A field line is a graphical visual aid for visualising vector fields.
- An electric field line is an imaginary line or curve drawn through a region of empty space so that its tangent at any point is in the direction of the electric field vector at that point.

- A field line consists of a directed line which is tangent to the field vector at each point along its length.

**What is electric field strength?**

**Electric field strength**

Electric field strength of an electric field at a given point in space is equal to the force the field would induce on a unit electric charge at the point.

**What do you mean by electric flux?**

**Electric flux**

- Electric flux is the measure of flow of the electric field through a given area.
- Electric flux refers to the electric field multiplied by the area of the surface projected in a plane and perpendicular to the field.
- Electric flux is proportional to the number of electric field lines going through a normally perpendicular surface.

**What do you mean by electric dipole moment?**

**Electric dipole moment**

- Electric dipole moment refers to a measure of the separation of positive and negative electrical charges within a system, that is, a measure of the system's overall polarity.
- Dipole moment is the mathematical product of the separation of the ends of a dipole and the magnitude of the charges (2a x q).

**What is electromagnetic wave?**

**Electromagnetic waves**

Electromagnetic waves or EM are waves that are created as a result of vibrations between an electric field and magnetic field.

**What is electromagnetic spectrum?**

**Electromagnetic spectrum**

The electromagnetic (EM) spectrum is the range of all types of EM radiation.

## What is electromagnetic radiation?

## Electromagnetic radiation

In physics, electromagnetic radiation refers to the waves of the electromagnetic field, propagating through space, carrying electromagnetic radiant energy.

## Define the electric potential difference.

## Electric potential difference

The electric potential difference is defined as the amount of work done to carry a unit charge from one point to another in an electric field.

## What do you mean by electrostatic potential (v) at a point?

## Electrostatic potential (v) at a point

- The electrostatic potential (V) at any point in a region with electrostatic field is the work done in bringing a unit positive charge (without acceleration) from infinity to that point.

- Work done by an external force in bringing a unit positive charge from infinity to a point is equal to electrostatic potential (v) at the point.

**What is electric power?**

**Electric power**

- Electric power is the rate, per unit time, at which electrical energy is transferred by an electric circuit.
- Electric power refers to the rate at which the work is being done in an electrical power.

**What is an electrolytic cell?**

**Electrolytic cell**

Electrolytic cell refers to a simple device used to maintain a steady current in an electric circuit.

**What is equipotential surface?**

**Equipotential surface**

- An equipotential surface is a surface with a constant value of potential at all points on the surface.
- In general, for any charge configuration, equipotential surface through a point is normal to the electric field at that point.

**What is electric current?**

**Electric current**

- Electric current is a stream of charged particles, such as electrons or ions, moving through an electrical conductor or space.
- Electric current is defined as the rate of flow of negative charges of the conductor.
- An electric current is flow of electric charge in a circuit.

# What is electric susceptibility of the dielectric medium?

## Electric susceptibility of the dielectric medium

- Electric susceptibility of the dielectric medium refers to the quantitative measure of the extent to which an electric field applied to a dielectric material causes polarization, the slight displacement of positive and negative charge within the material.

- The electric susceptibility of the dielectric material is a measure of how easily it polarizes in response to an electric field.

- The electric susceptibility determines the electric permittivity of the material and thus influences many other phenomenon in that medium, from the capacitance of capacitors to the speed of light.

## What do you mean by energy density of a capacitor?

**Energy density of a capacitor**

Energy density of a capacitor refers to the energy stored per unit volume of space.

**What do you mean by electrical energy?**

**Electrical energy**

- Electrical energy is a form of energy resulting from the flow of electric charge.
- Electrical energy is a form of kinetic energy.
- Electric energy is caused by moving electric charges called electrons.

**What is an electrochemical cell?**

**Electrochemical cell**

- An electrochemical cell is a device that generates electricity from a redox chemical reaction.
- An electrochemical cell is a device that converts chemical energy into electrical energy.

# What is electromotive force (e.m.f)of the cell?

## Electromotive force (e.m.f)

- The electromotive force (e.m.f) is the sum of the electric potential differences produced by a separation of charges (electrons or ions) that can occur at each phase boundary (or interface) in the cell.
- Electromotive force (e.m.f) is defined as the electric potential produced by either electrochemical cell or by changing the magnetic field.
- The electromotive force (e.m.f) of a cell is the maximum potential difference between two electrodes of a cell.
- The electromotive force (e.m.f) refers to the net voltage between the oxidation and reduction half-reactions.
- The electromotive force (e.m.f) is mainly used to determine whether an electrochemical cell is galvanic or not.

F

**Define the term field.**

**Field**

- Field, in physics, is a region in which each point is affected by a force.
- In physics, a field is a physical quantity, represented by a number, or a tensor, that has value for each point in space and time.
- Example, objects force to the ground because they are affected by the force of earth's gravitational field.

**What is focal length of the mirror?**

**Focal length of the mirror**

- The distance between the focus f and the pole p of the mirror is called the focal length of the mirror, denoted by 'f'.
- Mathematically, $f = r/2$ when 'r' is the radius of curvature of the mirror.


**G**

**What is galvanometer?**

A galvanometer is an electromechanical instrument used for detecting and indicating an electric current.

**What do you mean by grounding or earthing?**

**Grounding or earthing**

- Grounding or earthing refers to the process of sharing the charges with the earth.
- Earthing provides a safety measure for electrical circuits and appliances.

# I

**What are insulators?**

**Insulators**

Insulators are substances which offer high resistance to the passage of electricity through them.

**What do you mean by the image of the first point?**

**Image of the first point**

If rays emanating from a point actually meet at another point after reflection or refraction, that point is called the image of the first point.

**What is internal reflection of light?**

**Internal reflection of light**

When light travels from an optically denser medium to a rarer medium at the interface, it is partly reflected back into the same medium and partly refracted to the second medium. This reflection is called the internal reflection.

**What is internal resistance of a cell?**

**Internal resistance of a cell**

- Internal resistance of a cell refers to the opposition to the flow of current offered by the cells and batteries themselves resulting in the generation of heat.

- Internal resistance of a cell refers to the resistance offered by the electrolyte inside the cell to the flow of current.

# K

**What is kirchhoff's law and rule?**

Kirchhoff's laws quantify how current flow through a circuit and how voltage varies around a loop in a circuit.

**Junction rule**

**Kirchhoff's law (1st law)**

Kirchhoff's law states that current flowing into a node (or a junction) must be equal to current flowing out of it. This is a consequence of charge conservation

OR

At any junction, the sum of the currents entering the junction is equal to the sum of currents leaving the junction.

**Loop rule**

The algebraic sum of the changes in potential around any closed loop involving resistors and cells in the loop is zero.

# L

**What are like charges?**

**Like charges**

Like charges repel each other.

**What do you mean by line of force?**

**Line of force**

- Line of force refers to an imaginary line which represents the strength and direction of a magnetic, gravitational or electric field at any point.
- Line of force in Physics, path followed by an electric charge free to move in an

electric field or a mass free to move in an electric field  or mass free to move in a gravitational field or any appropriate test particle in a given force field .

**What is light in terms of optics?**

**Light**

- Light is an electromagnetic wave phenomenon described by the same theoretical principles that govern all forms of electromagnetic radiation.
- Optical frequencies occupy a band of the electromagnetic spectrum (wave length of about 400nm to 750nm) extends from the infrared through the visible to the ultraviolet.

**What is linear charge density?**

**Linear charge density**

Linear charge density is the quantity of charge per unit length at any point on a line charge distribution.

**What do you mean by linear isotropic dielectrics?**

**Linear isotropic dielectrics**

- A linear isotropic dielectric refers to a dielectric in which the permittivity is a scalar and has equal value at all direction.
- A dielectric whose polarization always has a direction that is parallel to the applied electric field and a magnitude which does not depend on the direction of the electric field.

**What is linear magnification?**

**Linear magnification**

Linear magnification (m) is defined as the ratio of the height of the image (h') to the height of the object (h).

Mathematically, $m = h'/h = -v/u$

**What is luminous intensity?**

**Luminous intensity**

- Luminous intensity refers to the luminous flux per unit solid angle.
- The luminous intensity refers to the quantity of visible light that is emitted in unit time per unit solid angle.
- The luminous intensity is a quantity for characterizing a light source.

**What is luminous flux?**

**Luminous flux or luminous power**

Luminous flux refers to the measure of the perceived power of light.

**What is lens?**

**Lens**

- A lens is a transmissive optical device that focuses or disperses a light beam by means of refraction.
- Lenses are made from material, such as glass or plastic, and are ground and polished or moulded to a desired shape.

- Lens is a clear curved piece of material (as glass) used to bend the rays of light to form an image.

# M

**What is meterbridge?**

**Meterbridge**

- A meter bridge is an instrument that works on the principle of a wheatstone bridge.
- A meter bridge is also called a slide wire bridge.
- A meter bridge is used in finding the unknown resistance of a conductor.

**What is mobility?**

**Mobility**

The mobility is defined as the magnitude of the drift velocity per unit electric field.

**What is mirage?**

- In optics, mirage refers to the deceptive appearance of a distant object or objects caused by the bending of light rays (refraction) in layers of air of varying density.
- A mirage is a naturally occurring optical phenomenon in which light rays bend via refraction to produce a displaced image of distant object or the sky.
- Mirages happen when the ground is very hot and the air is cool.

**What is magnification of a lens?**

**Magnification of a lens**

Magnification (m) produced by a lens refers to the ratio of the size of the image to that of the object.

**What is microscope?**

**Microscope**

A microscope is an instrument used to see objects that are too small to be seen by the naked eye.

# N

## What is negative charge?

**Negative charge**

Negative charge is a charge that has more electrons than protons and has a lower electrical potential.

# O

## What do you mean by one Ampere of current?

**One Ampere current**

One Ampere of current refers to the current that flows with electric charge of one Coulomb per second.

## What do you mean by one ohm?

**One ohm**

One ohm is defined as an electrical resistance between two points of a conductor when a constant potential difference of one volt, applied to these points, produces in the conductor a current of one Ampere, the conductor not being experiencing any electromotive force.

## What is optical density?

Optical density is the ratio of the speed of light in two media.

# P

## What are paraxial rays?

## Paraxial rays

A paraxial ray refers to a ray which makes a small angle to the optical axis of the system and lies close to the axis throughout the system.

## What is positive charge?

## Positive charge

- Positive charge means having a deficiency of electrons.
- Positive charge means having a higher electric potential.
- When an object has a positive charge, it means that it has more protons than electrons.

**What do you mean by polarity of charge?**

**Polarity of charge**

- Polarity of charge refers to the property which differentiates the two kinds of charges (positive charge or negative charge).
- Polarity is a term used in electricity, magnetism and electronic signalling.

**What is point charge in Physics?**

**Point charge**

A point charge is a hypothetical charge located at a single point in space.

## What do you mean by permittivity of free space?

### Permittivity of free space

- The permittivity of free space is a physical constant that represents the capability of a vacuum to permit electric fields.
- Permittivity of free space is often used in electromagnetism.
- Permittivity of free space is also connected to the energy stored within an electric field and capacitance.

## What do you mean by point dipole?

### Point dipole

- A point (electric) dipole is the limit obtained by letting the separation tend to 0 while keeping the dipole moment fixed.
- The dipole field at a point is inversely proportional to the cube of distance from the centre to the point. For a very small

dipole, the 2a approaches zero. This is called point dipole.

- A point dipole means the distance at which we are calculating electric field is much greater than the distance between the charges.

**Define potential energy differences in terms of the physically meaning for quantity work.**

**Potential energy differences**

The electric potential differences between points A and B, VB – VA, is defined to be the change in potential energy of a charge q moved from A to B, divided by the charge.

**Define potential energy of a test charge in terms of the work done on the charge.**

**Potential energy of a test charge**

- In an electrical circuit, the potential between two points (E) is defined as the amount of work done (w) by an external agent in moving a unit charge q from one point to another.

Mathematically, E = w/q.

- Potential energy of charge q at a point (in the presence of field due to any charge configuration) is the work done by the external force (equal and opposite to the electric force) in bringing the charge q from infinity to that point.

**What do you mean by potential due to a point charge?**

**Potential due to a point charge**

- Electric potential of a point charge is v= kq/r
- Electrostatic potential is scalar.

**What do you mean by potential due to a system of charge?**

**Potential due to a system of charges**

Potential at a point due to a system of charges is the sum of potentials due to individual charges.

Total potential, $V=V_1+ V_2+ V_3+ .........+ V_n$

**What is the potential energy of a single charge in an external field?**

**Potential energy of a single charge in an external field**

The potential energy of the charge q in the field is equal to the work done in bringing the charge from infinity to the point.

**What is the potential energy for a dipole in an external field?**

**Potential energy of a dipole in an external field**

Potential energy of a dipole placed in an external field is zero when the angle θ is equal to 90 or when the dipole makes an angle of 90.

**What is potentiometer?**

## Potentiometer

- A potentiometer is a three terminal resistor with a sliding or rotating contact that forms an adjustable voltage divider.
- Potentiometer is a device used to compare the e.m.f (electromotive force) of two cells, to measure the internal resistance of a cell, and potential difference across a resistor.
- Potentiometer works on zero deflection.
- Potentiometers are commonly used to control electrical devices such as volume controls on audio equipment.

## What is polarisation?

## Polarisation

Polarisation refers to the dipole moment per unit volume and is denoted by P.

## What is parallel plate capacitor?

A parallel plate capacitor is an arrangement that consists of two large plane parallel conducting plates separated by a small distance.

**What is polarisation of charge?**

**Polarisation of charge**

When a dielectric material is placed in the external electric field, then charge is induced in the dielectric material, hence an induced electric field is set up between the plates in the opposite direction to the external field. This is called polarization of the charge.

**What is principal axis of a concave or convex mirror?**

**Principal axis of a concave or convex mirror**

Principal axis of a concave or convex mirror refers to a line passing through the centre of the sphere and attaching to the mirror in the exact centre of the mirror.

**What is principal focus?**

## Principal focus

Principal focus refers to the point on the principal axis at which all the rays coming parallel to the principal axis appears to meet or diverge from it.

## What is a prism?

## Prism

A prism is an object made up of a transparent material, like glass or plastic that has at least two flat surfaces that form an acute angle (less than 90 degrees).

## What is power of a lens?

## Power of a lens

- Power of a lens is a measure of the convergence or divergence, which a lens introduced in the light falling on it.

Mathematically, $P=1/f$

- The power P of a lens is defined as the tangent of the angle by which it converges or diverges a beam of light parallel to the principal axis falling at unit distance from the optical centre.

## What is photometry?

## Photometry

Photometry refers to the measurement of light as perceived by human eye.

# Q

## What do you mean by quantisation of charge?

## Quantisation of charge

- Electric charge is always an integral multiple of e is termed as quantisation of charge.
- All free charges are integral multiples of a basic unit of charge denoted by e. Thus the charge q on a body is always given by $q = ne$.

- Quantisation of charge means that charge can take up only particular discrete values.

# R

**What is a ray of light?**

**Ray of light**

- A light ray is a line (straight or curved) that is perpendicular to the light's wavefronts, its tangent is collinear with the wave vector.
- The direction or path along which light energy travels in a medium is called a ray of light.

**What is Rayleigh scattering?**

Rayleigh scattering refers to the scattering of light by particles that are less than 1/15 of the wavelength of the light.

**What is reflection of light?**

**Reflection of light**

Reflection of light is the phenomenon of bouncing back of light in the same medium on striking the surface of any object.

## What do you mean by resistivity constant?

### Resistivity constant

Resistivity constant is quantitatively equal to the resistance R of a specimen such as a wire, multiplied by its cross sectional area A and divided by its length.

## What is refraction of light?

### Refraction

The direction of propagation of an oblique incident (0<i<90) ray of light that enters the other medium, changes at the interface of the two media. This phenomenon is called refraction of light.

## What do you mean by refractive index of the medium?

### Refractive index

- Refractive index of the medium is the measure of the bending of a ray of light when passing from one medium to another medium.
- Refractive index is also called index of refraction.
- Refractive index is a value calculated from the ratio of the speed of light in a vacuum to that in a second medium of greater density.

# S

## What are semiconductors?

## Semiconductors

- Semiconductors are the materials which have conductivity between conductors (generally metals) and non conductors or insulators (such as ceramics).
- Semiconductors can be compounds, such as gallium arsenide or pure elements, such as germanium or silicon.

**What do you mean by the term static in Physics?**

**Static**

- Static means anything that does not move or change with time.
- Static means stationary or at rest.

**What do you mean by source charge in an electric field?**

**Source charge in an electric field**

- Source charge in an electric field is a large charge through which electric fields flow.
- Source energy in an electric field the charge which is the cause of electric field in space.

**What do you mean by surface charge density?**

**Surface charge density**

- Surface charge density is the quantity of charge per unit area, at any point on surface charge distribution on a two dimensional surface.
- Surface charge density is a measure of how much electric charge is accumulated over a surface.

**What is a spherical mirror?**

**Spherical mirror**

A spherical mirror refers to the mirror whose reflecting surface is the part of a hollow sphere of glass.

**What is specular reflection of light?**

**Specular reflection of light**

Specular reflection of light refers to the light reflected from a smooth surface at a definite angle.

**What do you mean by series combination of resistors?**

## Combination of resistors in series

Two resistors are said to be in series if only one of their end points is joined.

## What is scattering of light?

## Scattering of light

- Scattering of light is the phenomenon in which light rays get deviated from its straight path on striking an obstacle like dust or molecules, water vapour etc.

- Scattering of light gives rise to many spectacular phenomenon such as Tyndall effect and the "red hues of sunrise and sunset ".

## What is rainbow?

- A rainbow is meteorological phenomenon that is caused by reflection, refraction and dispersion of light in water droplets resulting in a spectrum of light appearing in the sky.

- Rainbow takes the form of a multicoloured circular arc.

# T

**What is test charge?**

**Test charge**

A test charge is the charge used to test the effect of an electric filed.

**What do you mean by test charge in an electric field?**

**Test charge in an electric field**

- Test charge in an electric field is a small electropositive charge used for experiments.
- A test charge is a positive charge of very small magnitude which gives the direction and strength of electric field in space without influencing the electric field.

**What do you mean by temperature co-efficient of resistivity?**

**The temperature co- efficient of resistance**

The temperature co- efficient of resistance refers to the change in electrical resistance of a substance with respect to per degree change in temperature.

**What is total internal reflection?**

**Total internal reflection**

Total internal reflection refers to a complete reflection of a ray of light within a medium such as water or glass from the surrounding surfaces back into the medium. The phenomenon occurs if the angle of incidence is greater than a certain limiting angle, called the critical angle.

**What is telescope?**

**Telescope**

A telescope is an optical instrument using lenses, curved mirrors or a combination of both to observe distant object or various devices used to observe distant objects by them emission, absorption or reflection of electromagnetic radiation.

## U

**What are unlike charges?**

**Unlike charges**

Unlike charges attract each other.

## V

**What is volume charge density?**

**Volume charge density**

Volume charge density is the quantity of charge per unit volume at any point in a volume.

## W

**What is wire bound resistors?**

## Wire bound resistors

Wire bound resistors are made by winding the wires of an alloy i.e manganin, constantan and nichrome.

## What is wheat stone bridge?

- A wheat stone bridge is an electrical circuit used to measure an unknown electrical resistance by balancing two legs of a bridge circuit, one leg of which includes the unknown component.
- The wheat stone bridge provides extremely accurate measurements.
- Wheat stone bridge is an electrical bridge consisting of two branches of a parallel circuit joined by a galvanometer and used for determining the value of an unknown resistance in one of the branches.
- A wheatstone bridge works on the principal of null deflection, which means the ratio of their resistances are equal and hence no current flows through the circuit.

# SI units

## 1. Write the SI unit of charge.

The SI unit of charge is called Coulomb and is denoted by the symbol C.

## 2. Write the SI unit of permittivity of free space.

The SI unit of permittivity of free space is $N^{-1}m^{-2}C^2$.

## 3. Write the SI unit of electric charge.

The SI unit of electric charge is volt per meter (V/m).

## 4. Write the SI unit of electric flux.

SI unit of electric flux is volt meter (Vm) or equivalently $Nm^2C^{-1}$.

## 5. Write the SI unit of electric dipole moment.

The SI unit of electric dipole moment is the Coulomb-meter.

**6. Write the SI unit of surface charge density.**

The SI unit of surface charge density is $Cm^{-2}$.

**7. Write the SI unit of linear charge density.**

The SI unit of linear charge density is $Cm^{-1}$.

**8. Write the SI unit of volume charge density.**

The SI unit of volume charge density is $Cm^{-3}$.

**9. Write the SI unit of electric current.**

The SI unit of electric current is Ampere.

**10. Write the SI unit of resistance.**

The SI unit of resistance is Ohm.

**11. Write the SI unit of resistivity.**

The SI unit of resistivity is Ohm-meter.

**12. Write the SI unit of current density.**

The SI unit of current density is $A/m^2$.

**13. Write the SI unit of mobility.**

The SI unit of mobility is $m^2/SV$

**14. Write the SI unit of luminous intensity.**

The SI unit of luminous intensity (I) is candela (cd).

**15. Write the SI unit for power of lens.**

Dioptre(d)

**16. Write the SI unit of electric power.**

The SI unit of electric power is the watt, one joule per second.

## Short Question and Answer

**1. What are the basic properties of electric charge?**

**The basic properties of electric charges are:**

- Electric charge is the physical property of matter that causes it to experience a force when placed in an electromagnetic field.

- There are two types of electric charge, positive and negative (commonly carried by protons and electrons respectively).

- Like charges repel each other and unlike charges attract each other.

- Additivity of charges ---- charges add up like real numbers or they are scalars like the mass of a body. If the system contains n charges $q1, q2, \ldots\ldots\ldots, q_n$ then the total charge of the system is $q1 + q2 + \ldots\ldots\ldots + q_n$.

- Charge is conserved ------ the total charge of the isolated system is always conserved.

- Quantisation of charge

## 2. What are the three laws of electric charge?

**The three laws of electric charges are:**

- Opposite charges attract each other.

- Like charges repel each other.
- Charged objects attract neutral objects.

## 3. Write the first law of electrostatics.

- Like charges repel each other and unlike charges attract each other.
- The first law tells only about the nature of force i.e repulsive or attractive.

## 4. State Coulomb's law.

### Coulomb's law

- Coulomb's law states that "the magnitude of the electrostatic force of attraction or repulsion between two point charges is directly proportional to the product of the magnitudes of charges and inversely proportional to the square of the distance between them."
- If two point charges $q_1$, $q_2$ are separated by a distance r in vacuum , the magnitude of the force F between them is given by

$$F = k\,|q_1 * q_2|/r^2$$

# 5. State Gauss's law.

## Gauss law

- Gauss law states that the total electric flux out of a closed surface is equal to the charge enclosed divided by the permittivity.
- Gauss's law states that the electric flux through any closed surface is proportional to the total electric charge enclosed by the surface.
- Gauss's law for the electric field describes the static electric field generated by a distribution of electric charges.

# 6. State Ohm's law.

## Ohm's law

- Ohm's law states that the current through a conductor between two points is directly proportional to the voltage applied to it.

- Mathematically, $V=IR$, in the equation, the constant of proportionality, R is resistance.
- Ohm's law states that the strength of a direct current is directly proportional to the potential difference and inversely proportional to the resistance of the circuit.
- Ohm's law gives the relationship between current, voltage and resistance.

## 7. Write the principle of superposition.

### The principle of superposition

The principle of superposition states that every charge in space creates an electric field at point independent of the presence of other charges in that medium.

## 8. What are the four important properties of electric field lines?

### Properties of an electric field are:

- Field lines never inter sect each other.

- They are perpendicular to the surface charge.
- The field is strong when the lines are close together, and it is weak when the field lines move apart from each other.
- The number of field lines is directly proportional to the magnitude of the charge.

## 9. What does electric field lines represent?

Electric field lines reveal information about the direction (and the strength) of an electric field within a region of space.

## 10. Write the physical significance of dipole.

### Physical significance of dipole

- Dipole is used to predict whether a molecule is polar or non polar.
- Dipole gives a measure of the polarity/ polarization of a net neutral system.

## 11. What are the types of electromagnetic radiation?

Electromagnetic radiation includes radio waves, microwaves, infrared, light, ultraviolet, x-rays and gamma rays.

## 12. What do you mean by potential due to an electric dipole?

**Potential due to an electric dipole**

$V = 4\pi\epsilon r_2 PCos\theta$ where,

P is the dipole moment

r is the distance at which the potential V of the dipole is calculated

$\theta$ is the angle between the distance vector and the dipole

## 13. Write the relation between electric field and potential.

- Electric field is in the direction in which the potential decreases steepest.

- Electric field magnitude is given by the change in the magnitude of potential per unit displacement normal to the equipotential surface at the point.

## 14. What is the value for minimum and maximum potential energy for a dipole?

- When the angle between the dipole moment and electric field is 180 then the potential energy of electric dipole is maximum.
- When the angle between the dipole moment and electric field is zero then the potential energy of electric dipole is minimum.

## 15. What are the types of spherical mirror?

Spherical mirror are of two types:

- Concave mirror
- Convex mirror

## 16. Write two types of the reflection of light.

Two types of the reflection of light are:

- Specular reflection of light
- Diffused reflection of light

## 17. Write the application of potentiometer.

- Potentiometer is used to compare the e.m.f 's of different cells.
- Potentiometer is used as a variable resistor in most of applications.
- Potentiometer is used to control stereo audio volume.

## 18. Write the effects of dielectric on capacitance.

Introducing a dielectric into a capacitor decreases the electric field, which decreases the voltage, which increases the capacitance.

## 19. Write two types of commercially produced resistors.

Commercially produced resistors for domestic use or in laboratories are of two major types: wire bound resistors and carbon resistors.

**20. Give few examples of material that exhibit a very weak dependence of resistivity with temperature.**

Nichrome (an alloy of nickel, iron and chromium), Manganin and constantan.

**21. Write the relation between the resistivity of semiconductors with temperature.**

The resistivity of semiconductors decreases with increasing temperature.

**22. Write the condition for an image to be real or virtual.**

- The image is real if the rays actually converge to the image of first point.

- The image is virtual, if the rays do not actually meet but appear to diverge from the point when produced backwards.

## 23. What happens when the ray from the point which is parallel to the principal axis?

The reflected ray goes through the focus of the mirror.

## 24. What happen when the ray passing through the centre of curvature of a concave mirror or appearing to pass through it for a convex mirror?

The reflected ray simply retraces the path.

## 25. What happens to the ray passing through (or directed towards) the focus of the concave mirror or appearing to pass through (or directed towards) the focus of a convex mirror?

The reflected ray is parallel to the principal axis.

**26. What happens when the ray is incident at any angle at the pole?**

The reflected ray follows law of reflection.

**27. Write some important result regarding electrostatic of conductors.**

**Some important results are:**

- Inside a conductor, electrostatic field is zero.
- At the surface of a charged conductor, electrostatic field must be normal to the surface at every point.
- The interior of a conductor can have no excess charge in the static situation.
- Electrostatic potential is constant throughout the volume of the conductor and has the same value (as inside) on its surface.
- Electric field at the surface of a charged conductor is $E=\sigma n/\varepsilon_0$
- Electrostatic shielding

**28. Write the laws of refraction of light.**

**The laws of refraction of light are:**

- The incident ray, the refracted ray and the normal to the interface at the point of incidence all lie in the same plane.
- The ratio of the sine of the angle of incidence to the sine of the angle of refraction is constant.

Mathematically, sin i/sin r $=n_{21}$

## 29. When a refracted ray bends towards the normal?

If $n_{21}>1$ and r<i. In this case, medium 2 is said to be optically denser than one medium1.

## 30. Why diamond shows spectacular brilliance?

Diamond brilliance is mainly due to the total internal reflection of light inside them.

## 31. Name the object that exhibit total internal reflection.

Diamond, prism and optical fibre.

## 32. What are the main physical quantities in photometry?

- The luminous intensity of the source
- The luminous flux or flow of light from the source .
- Illuminance of the surface

## 33. Name some devices that use combination of their lenses in contact.

A system of combination of lenses is commonly used in designing lenses for cameras, microscopes, telescopes etc.

## 34. When wheat stone bridge is in unbalanced condition?

Under normal condition, the bridge will be in the unbalanced condition where current flows through the galvanometer.

## 35. When wheatstone bridge is in balanced condition?

The bridge will be in a balanced condition when no current flows through the galvanometer.

**36. Name some optical devices and instruments that have been designed using reflecting and refracting properties of the mirrors, lenses and prisms.**

Periscope, kaleidoscope, binoculars, telescope and microscopes.

**37. Write differences between terrestrial telescope and astronomical telescope.**

**Astronomical telescope**

- Astronomical telescopes are used for viewing distant stars and planets.
- The final image in the astronomical telescope is inverted.

**Terrestrial telescope**

- Terrestrial telescope are used for viewing distant objects on earth.

- The final image in the terrestrial telescope is erect.